Memento Mori

a book of sonnets

poems by

M. Brooke Wiese

Finishing Line Press
Georgetown, Kentucky

Memento Mori

a book of sonnets

For Mindee and Benjamin and Theo

ACKNOWLEDGMENTS

"The Night Buses" and "Meditation on Time and Space" appeared in *Qutub Minar Review*.

"Early Spring, Central Park," "Three White Swans," "Sometimes at 4:00 AM the Moon," "Late December Storm," "Pigeons," and "Words" appeared in *Poem*.

"Memento Mori" appeared in *Sparks of Calliope*.

"This Day, This Night," and "Reminders of Death Abound" appeared in The *Orchards Poetry Journal*.

"And You Left Me Deep in My Emotions" appeared in *Literature Today: An International Journal*.

"Morphine" appeared in *The Chained Muse*.

"In the Waiting Room at a Famous Cancer Hospital," and "Cleaning the Refrigerator" appeared in *Pulsebeat Poetry Journal*.

"My Parents, Now Living in a Petrarchan Sonnet" appeared in *Spoon River Poetry Review*.

"New York Tenement Rooftop," and "Prospero's Epilogue" appeared in Bronze Bird Books *Tiny Moments* and anthologies.

"The City, Derelict" appeared in *The Poetry Porch*.

Publisher: Leah Huete de Maines
Editor: Christen Kincaid
Cover Art: Still Life with Skull, Paul Cézanne, public domain
Author Photo: M. Brooke Wiese
Cover Design: Elizabeth Maines McCleavy

Order online: www.finishinglinepress.com
also available on amazon.com

Author inquiries and mail orders:
Finishing Line Press
PO Box 1626
Georgetown, Kentucky 40324
USA

Contents

The Treefort

Once, long ago, we climbed to a fort
high in a tree in the New England woods behind
your very big house with its treelined
drive and swimming pool and tennis court,
and a mother who made us lemonade, and a real sport
of a dad. I had made up my mind
to learn to kiss and you weren't disinclined,
and so that heady summer we did disport.

Once, up in the treefort in the wood
behind your house, with someone's father's girlie
magazines, all curvy hips and breasts and pearly
teeth, we giggled and made rude
jokes, full of knowing swagger. We graffitied
mustaches and other things on every
airbrushed nude, practiced talking dirty
and laughed at jokes we feigned we understood.

You were in your soccer shorts and cleats
and I in denim cutoffs, a striped shirt
I liked a lot, and pigtails I did not.
This sounds like a simple tale of boy meets
girl, and it's true, we *did* flirt,
and consort, and there was exquisite heat

where your knuckles brushed my breast buds or I pressed,
in passing, against your white fly-front jeans,
but I wanted to be like you, a boy,
and you wanted to be Ursula Andress,
and I longed for the women in those magazines,
so unlike my mother—oh, joy!

Animal Dreams

She dreams she is an ocelot, sleek
and stripey, spotted like a mackerel,
lithe and loopy. Favorite meal: meat.
Favorite matter: preternatural.

She dreams *he* is a sea otter, wet
and snaky. Slurping urchins, he flips and glides,
cracks clamshells with a rock on his belly fat.
He smells of seaweed, mollusks and tides.

In her dreams they are circling in moonlight,
high in the cobalt air like a Chagall painting. She brightens
and devours a carcass. Under planets and starlight
they frolic like kittens. The universe stretches and heightens.

Jolted awake by her buzzing phone
she assesses her human body, alone.

Prospero's Epilogue

My son is learning Prospero's epilogue
for school and I help him practice. He has to memorize
his lines, present his monologue
in class. I try to help him analyze

this soliloquy from Shakespeare's final play, about mercy.
Is it easy for an inward-turned fourteen-year-old boy
to put himself in the sandals of a wheezy
old man? I try to imagine myself that boy

imagining himself old and looking into the abyss
at life's end. I try to imagine what
he sees from his perspective—his life vigorous
and without end—but I cannot.

Asleep, he's curled around his orange cat.
It's something about forgiveness, I remember that.

Curtal Sonnet for a Teenaged Son

(after Gerard Manley Hopkins)

My teenaged son—the one with dark brown fuzz
above the farthest edges of his lips, like moss,
as if he'd drawn it on with my eyebrow pencil
and who, with his luxurious brows and pompadour, does
right now resemble Mexico's comic hero, Cantinflas,
an honor lost on him with his resentful
glares and surly stares—is the sun.

Elaborate and imprecise as a Rococo blunderbuss,
he tilts at windmills, pushes the mule
up the slope, only to have it run back down
                    the hill.

Sometimes at 4:00 AM the Moon

Sometimes at 4:00 a.m. the moon—a waning quarter
passing through the dark sky, a barque with butter-colored
sails, square-rigged, stacked and moonsail topped—
navigates the strait where night meets day.

This window frames me; the moon details the park
below in silhouette, tree by tree. Bark
and bench and ballpark, bole and branch and root,
knotweed, chicory, wild violets, arrowroot.

Central Park's resplendent in the moonlight.
Parked cars glow under buttery streetlight.
I stand at my window looking out, alone.
Ah, but you are there, *amorette*,

asleep behind me, and it's a long shot *darling*,
whether or not we'll still be "we" come morning.

And You Left Me Deep in My Emotions

How many houseflies died while we stepped crosswise,
one foot over the other, in front, in back,
traversing life's stage on a sideways track
in a *pas de bourrée*, imbalanced. And what is *always*
anyway for a housefly? For a woman? How
does each value a relationship, a marriage, sex?
Am I less valuable as your ex?
Fraught words: vow, avow, hausfrau,
plough, spouse, force, arouse, buss, both,
seduce, abuse, mouth, us, troth.
What is the measure of a woman's life
against that of a housefly, an Immortal Jellyfish,
or a planet birthed in a primordial broth?
And to a woman, to a housefly, what is time? What is love?

The Gun Sonnets

(1965/2015)

I. Skin

When his skin broke flying over
the chrome handlebars—his face erasing
the roadstripe, split and forever
spliced at seven like a Picasso painting facing
left and right at once—they called him braver
than those first astronauts. He stopped debasing
himself eventually, and whenever
his husband touched his face he felt a blessing.

When his skin broke at least twenty-four
times and unfixable, more than half
in his back, he cried out in his head
for his mother who'd always soothed him before,
and felt something hiss when they called him black,
and when they couldn't fix him he was dead.

II. Bone

Sliding hard into second base
he felt his cleat strike the bag as he broke
his hometown record for stolen bases,
but his heyday ended with a crack,
the bone poking through the skin and the wan faces
of his parents in the stands, horror-struck
and stuck to their seats. But time minimizes
pain and turns the pages of Life's book.

A sharp crack and a percussive pock-pock-pock
as the bone is struck and his leg shorn right off
above the calf and he'll never have two feet
again, but he feels lucky, taking stock,
for though the bone was pulverized like chaff,
those around him on the ground were mincemeat.

III. Blood

When we were wild and innocent at once—
at seven or eight, but not yet nine,
unencumbered by our innocence,
unburdened by grown-up things and intertwined
like double helix strands—we swore allegiance
with a puncture from a rose's thorn,
comingling our blood, then sucked a fingertip, convinced
the taste of iron in the wound was wine.

Sometimes the wound is clean if the lone shooter
is experienced and true—the hole is but a dimple,
and like ink on fine rag paper there's a discrete
bleed. But this is what we know when still sober:
The first trooper is too late. Small cutouts are crumpled
on the floor around him. The room smells musky and sweet.

Year of the Comet

...whose leaders preached that suicide would allow them to leave their bodily "containers" and enter an alien spacecraft hidden behind the Hale-Bopp comet.

On April first, nineteen ninety-seven,
I wheeled my father down the gravel drive
to our cul-de-sac; his uneasy expression
wrenched my heart, but I wanted to give

him this gift before he left this earth,
and me. I braked his chair, leaned over his ear
and pointed, *Look up!* We watched the bright comet traverse
the sky on my birthday. It slowly roamed the mesosphere

that year he slowly left it. In pictures
from the San Diego mansion, men and women slept
in bunkbeds in matching tracksuits and new sneakers,
with quarters in their pockets to call their mothers, who wept

over bodies, cool as clay—whose children's fate
was to ride the tail of a comet to Heaven's Gate.

In the Waiting Room at a Famous Cancer Hospital

Out of the rumbling ground and into the bright
August light, into the city scrum,
the gum-covered sidewalks, the human bloom,
the lack of air and elbow room, the blight
in streets where rats and pigeons fight
for crumbs or top-dog status, the scaffolding a boon
only in a storm. Out of the shout and out of the din,
the waiting room is almost too polite.

Heavy curtains drawn against the daylight
mute the voices in the waiting room
to a soft *ssh-ssh*, like a broom
sweeping. The carpet's pattern is infinite;
the low pile guaranteed to accommodate
a cane or walker. The walls are pale as the moon.
The unassuming art is laudanum
for the sick, unobjectionable as life.

You might expect a moan from those with no
hope left, or those alone and lonely. Instead
you'll find a convivial place where people nod
and smile in passing, yet keep contained as though
a broad gesture or loud guffaw might offend;
and all are patient, and no one finds it odd.

There's coffee too, and tea (for free!) and no
lack of crackers to nibble by patients with hatted heads
for stomachs distressed by the fusillade
of poisons shot into a vein, a salvo
against the spread of errant cells, the *Red
Devil* entrenched in a battle to the death with God.

Lacrimosa

(J.A.W.)

In the beginning I leapt from you,
and in my mouth I could feel
the dull ache of you like a sore tooth.

In my youth I flew from you, wheeling
like a seagull, away. A barnacle,
you clung to my hull, appealing.

In the end, my mouth was full
of words, but too wooly to spit
even one out; nor could I pull

the answers I needed from your magic hat.
We sat silent in a cool blue room.
But it had mostly been like that.

This is your doomsday, not mine yet.
Ten thousand and ten thousand days, my debt.

Morphine

for my mother

The nurse thumbs the wheel that opens the tube
that releases that exquisite lube

that bathes the sere and crumbling hummocks of your brain
and flushes out the tatters of your pain.

As you soak up that magical juice
your sinews, skin and links get loose

and you forget, first me, and then your cat
and you're no longer sitting there where you sat.

With Lethe's sweet water in your veins
you depopulate—college roommates, names

of childhood friends, an illicit lover,
teachers, bosses, my father, and last, your own mother,

all emptying into the vortex oblivion.
Irresistible. Final. Elysium.

My Parents, Now Living in a Petrarchan Sonnet

I wonder where they are now, my mother
and father, who moved with my sister westward to the Pacific
with her second husband, to be there for the beatific
birth of their first great-grandchild from my sister's daughter

and her daughter's wife. They are squatters,
my parents, settling in, parasitic
even, taking up more than their specific
space in the cupboard. Lollygaggers and hoggers.

They are old, and white as bone china,
white as bone, dusty as hearth ash,
papery and brittle as a late-Autumn leaf
riddled with pinholes, yet dense as manna
in twin cardboard boxes, still clannish,
still stealing our love like a thief.

Words

*"Adult native test-takers learn almost one new word a day
until middle age."*
—The Economist

Age does not glide in like a swan,
but like a flat-bottomed scow, a leaden,
broad-beamed, blunt-bowed punt, a rusted ton
of floating iron ore, its prow battered, hold laden.

At the end of a high-speed car chase,
the inevitable crash into lamppost or tree—
the accordion-pleated hood and the brain in its braincase
rattling around like the seedpods of a Flamboyant tree.

I am losing at least one word a day,
usually two or more. By week's end, a score
of names and tip-of-the-tongue things gone. Grey
matter in disarray. A trapdoor
opens and they all fall out.
Would that finger-strings had more clout.

Memento Mori

In my kitchen, musing on Cézanne's Still Life with Skull *(1898)*

Apples, oranges and pears fill the bowl,
bananas and grapes spill over its lip;
the footed bowl is cinnabar, jewel-
like against the black walnut tabletop
burnished by a hundred years of eating.
It is an uneventful scene, and ours
is a modest home. Life is fleeting.
Many days I hear Charon's oars
thunk against the oarlocks as he slowly
rows dead souls across the River Styx,
their mouth-coins his recompense. Such folly
to think I can escape with either promises or tricks
when even luscious fruit, if forgotten,
shrivels, molders, leaks, and grows rotten.

Meditation on Time and Space

I spread my fingers to the sky and frame
the full moon, a bright, milky white
marble between my forefinger and thumb.
I wish I could as easily reach the height

of moon and stars as I appear to hold
the heavens in my hand. Where do *I*
begin and end, as I am star-stuff, old
as everything—acid, alkali—

agnostic molecules of salt and water.
Is my boundary where I touch my skull,
and me inside, or am I one with other
matter, my mind merely a vehicle

to other places, expanding, unconfined
by time or space, with no demarcation line.

Early Spring, Central Park

For months bare branches beat against a grey
sky, everything so tightly wrapped.
Demeter's revenge for Persephone's
abduction to the Underworld, earth sapped

and fallow. It seems so simple the way things bloom—
inevitable how, after a soaking rain
followed by a day of vernal sun,
the willows' leaves unfurl in palest green,

then burst forth like fireworks. A fecund surge
follows: forsythia's yellow halo, hills and dells
of daffodils, magnolia, bleeding heart and spurge.
Pussy willow, buttercup, red maple, bluebells.

Demeter now keeps her daughter housebound,
implores her to stay nine months above ground.

Hell Gate

Here, with the horizontal movement impeded by the
opposite flow of the Harlem River and the narrowness of
the channel up to the Sound, the huge basin of the Hell
Gate begins to fill. The waters, like wild beasts, circle their
confines, impatient for the chance to escape.

Clouds slide over the river like giant
tortoises—they amble, high-
domed and slow, with psoriatic feet,
and gambol over the water roiling below.

Churning eddies push a wall of water
north along the river's banks and crash
into the tidal current sucking south,
to empty back into the river's mouth.

Three waterways, pushed and pulled
by restless tides collide. It would be
a thrill to ride the river spilling over
smoothly polished river stones in brackish
water full of sailors' bones and boys, escaping schools,
who disappeared into whirlpools.

Two COVID Couplet Sonnets, Blue and Black

Our world has reached a heart-wrenching milestone.
—António Guterres, United Nations secretary general

I. Ship's Log, January 15, 2020: At Sea

I dreamed I went to sea to see the world.
I watched as the waves curled and uncurled.

I had with me only a sea bag
filled with stones, and four gills of grog.

I'm kidding. I feasted on fear and grief every night
with the captain, and raised a glass to life. At midnight

on deck in the moonlight I thought of you and sent you a text
via WhatsApp, and reflected on my next

port as I studied each chart and map. With my smartwatch
and a translation program I hopscotched

around the world and came to understand the yin and yang
of it, but something had upset the hang

of it, as if the world had lost its gravity.
Around me, all at sea, everyone floated to infinity,

II. Wild Blue Yonder (Lost in Space)

up and up into the ether, light as a feather.
In the stratosphere there is no weather

so there was nothing to hold the people back
as they lifted up into the air that was so blue at first, then black,

the *wild blue yonder's* stratification.
Some cried out for their mothers, and some *huzzahed* with
   anticipation

as they ascended to the edge of everything,
tear-streaked faces full of wonder or misgiving,

one by one, twomillionsouls leaked
from the exosphere and were excreted

into outer space, half-way to the moon.
I pulled a stone from my sea bag, carved with Odin's rune,

and placed it on a marble tomb; two million gone.
How soon to reach a hundred million? What have we done?

Reminders of Death Abound

In galleries reminders of death abound
at the Metropolitan Museum of Art
filled with paintings of a stick-like man crowned
with thorns, beneath a sword and fiery heart,

lying limp across his mother's lap.
And on the wall in another hall
are paintings of fruit—luscious, lush, ripe—
with a mallard duck and a hare, and an oyster shell

on the table in front of the bowl of fruit. The hare's
fur so life-like you want to touch it, wonder if you can,
but the shell is empty, nothing there,
and the rabbit and duck are as limp as the languid man.

Look closely at the deep purple plum
that's past its prime. Note the alabaster worm.

The Night Buses

The buses pass at night heading north
along the park, almost empty, one
after another. Sometimes there's no one
but the driver, last man on earth.
I can see right in from my fourth
floor window; bathed in tungsten halogen
the passengers sit still as stone,
straight-jacketed in their plastic berth.

I have not yet ridden a plague bus,
but some people have no choice,
like the driver of the bus of course,
and the grocery store clerk, and the nurse
in scrubs, and the man who's standing, just in case,
heading home to his family from his workplace.

The City, Derelict

*The largest store of gold in the world is in the underground vaults
of the New York Federal Reserve Bank.*

At Louise Nevelson Plaza where Maiden Lane
meets William Street, in the long black shadow
of the towering flat black monochromatic
silhouettes, stark against the wan

December sky, here, where the few afflict
the many and the monied mingle with the haven't any,
here, where there's sun but it's never sunny
on the cobbled streets of the city derelict,

a pile of carefully folded blankets rests against
the sculpture's broad base, tucked there for cover
with the tenderness of a mother or a new lover—
the trappings of a life condensed.

Across the street the Federal Reserve Bank
looks down—stone-faced, stolid, blank.

The City from My Rooftop in July

Silver-painted rooftops reflect heat
up and away to cool the apartments below,
but the hot wind meets my face like a blow
and the soft tar paper under my feet
is like the rolling motion of a street
in an earthquake. Look down and risk vertigo,
but look out and the city stretches on and on: a tableau
where Matchbox cabs and buses cross but rarely meet.

All across the rooftops vents line up
like sentries in a row, and wooden water towers
built a hundred years ago fill up
then flow with gravity's magic pull to sinks and showers
in flats below. And Downtown, the slimmest towers pierce
the clouds, heading for outer space.

Pigeons

A thrum of beating wings. A flock of pigeons
rises suddenly, sweeps up the chimney
of tall and stalwart buildings gazing grimly
across the avenues. At the island's edges, bridges
lead to succor or affliction: commute
at your peril. Cars honk and some noisome smell
bedevils everyone. The pigeons whorl
like a cyclone in a water bottle—a fugue,
a contrapuntal composition, *this*,
then *that*, interwoven. The subway is a metal
marvel. This city, pinned down
in Manhattan Schist and Fordham Gneiss,
is everything. Just as abruptly they settle,
still as the pavement, huddled on the building's crown.

Flaco, Thriving

*Flaco, a Eurasian Eagle-Owl, escaped from the Central
Park Zoo when vandals cut a hole in his cage. The keepers
tried, unsuccessfully, to lure him back to the zoo. They
worried he would not know how to feed himself and would
die, but he learned to fly and to hunt New York City rats,
a plentiful food supply.*

Across the street in Central Park an owl
is preening, primping on a branch way up
above the crowd of people looking up
at him; haughty princeling scowling down

upon his star-struck hangers-on. No fowl
is he, but raptor, we (for I am there
beneath his tree) with long lenses peer
through leafy branches for a smile. His guile

drew Pallas Athena to make him her consort.
He has no truck with us. He makes sport
of the brown rat, his favorite meat,
available on every city street.
Huge and hungry, winging round the Harlem Meer,
he dreams of taking down a small deer.

* *After a year in the wild, Flaco ultimately succumbed from ingesting
life-threatening levels of rat poison.*

Wildebeests

Like all New Yorkers, wildlife living in urban areas love to explore their city.
　　　　　　—from the New York City Parks Urban
　　　　　　Wildlife Calendar

My city is enamored with the raptors
taking up residence in Central Park
or peering down from cliff-like aeries of granite, brick,
and brownstone all along the Avenues. These adaptors
feast on fat rodents full of rye bread
and pastrami, pizza and cupcakes
dropped in the grass by children whose bellies ache,
overfed at *al fresco* birthday parties and picnic spreads.

A red-tailed hawk catches an updraft and glides
around the pond on rising thermals, casting
its eye earthward for dinner; he larks about and rubbernecks.
Interloping foxes, possums and soft-eyed
deer are already here, and rumor has it
coyotes are even now headed downtown from the Bronx.

Police Blotter: Late July

Kentucky bluegrass laid down last
spring as sod has taken nicely; it's thick
and deep under my shoulders. The bedrock
below roots this striving, glass-faced
city where I flatten and recast
myself until I become the earth: sweet and black
and loamy. Sycamore, Sweetgum, Mulberry, Oak
and Black Cherry march along the meadow's crest.

Clouds scud across the sky and I
am suddenly awash in bright, white
moonlight, so that someone walking by
with quickened step and nervous eye would take fright
at seeing me asleep under the canopy—
old white lady—strange tableau at midnight.

New York Tenement Rooftop

August nights, and the black tarpaper roof
still holds the day's sun. Our tangled limbs,
the air finally cooling, the pigeon coup
quiet now, pigeons cooing pigeon hymns

softly. In the morning they will fly
aloft in a gyre before coming back
to settle on the rooftop. White, grey,
brown, black, mottled, they react

to something we can't see—a dragonfly,
feathers ruffled by a light breeze,
a red-tailed hawk circling. We lie
beneath the water tower in our memories.

Sunrise: looking down the avenue, a lesson
in perspective, the moon a fading crescent.

Cleaning the Refrigerator

The fettuccine from that night we both
were angry, fought, stayed up late. Then, granting clemency,
made love, cooked, and ate. I dump an overgrowth
of mold—a bowl-shaped pasta filigree.

I toss something sour, and pale as a spleen.
In the fruit bin, a jungle: a dusky blue
plum, dusted with a dry grey soot. A nectarine,
bruised and blooming. And greens, a gluey stew.

A lone silver pickle swims in a milky film.
A party goat cheese I forgot, or didn't want,
now black and rotting. And something totally unknown
clots the sink like cottage cheese, redolent

and overwhelming. Mouth-breathing, I hold my nose
against the stink as slowly I, too, decompose.

Late December Storm

(Barnegat Bay)

The bay is dark matter, swallowing lights
on the farther shore; the frigid chop obscures
in narrow furrows pale flights of stars,
distant planets, winking satellites…

A waxing gibbous moon is mostly hidden
by ink-dropped-into-water towering thunderclouds;
voluminous as funeral shrouds
they blot out silhouettes of mast and mizzen.

Yesterday the wind shook my neighbor's
old yew tree by its roots and threw
it in the bay without remorse. Who
am I to ask for small favors—

like longer days or an early spring—
when this bitter wind makes my old house sing?

Three White Swans

Three white swans have settled in,
paddling every morning in a line
across the bay like proud doyennes in flowered
hats gliding into court, oblivious
to the laughing gulls or the jay
who scolds them from my rooftop where he holds
a long view of today's regatta on the bay.

Once, they took off running, wings outstretched,
feet splayed and slapping wavetops, necks
reaching for the sky, as if to fly.

They ran across the swells for twenty paces
then, just like that, they sat back down,
their wakes intersecting in the channel
like a Venn diagram.

Loveladies

(Women About to Return, *1972 oil on canvas,*
by Nicaraguan painter Armando Morales)

Three ladies on the beach at dusk.
Three ladies sat or leaned or stood,
pink and rich as lobster bisque.
Three ladies, neither bad nor good.

Languorously they stood or sat
or leaned their amplitude like that
after practicing their arabesques,
naked and musky, amidst the driftwood.

Each lady slowly turned her mask
into the last sun to bask before returning home,
and in someone else's breast, belly, buttocks, limb—
in someone else's name, like *Seraphim*
or *Almudena Queen of Tamarind,*
posed like an odalisque.

This Day, This Night

Across the bay at night lights shine
and glitter along the mainland shore like
far-away planets and stars. Buoy bells strike
and chime, a tone poem atop the waves. A line

of towers flashes morse-code patterns known
only to skippers heading to the dark
sea to fish. Each beacon is a landmark.
Each transmitter blinking says you're not alone.

Earlier we linked arms along the beach
collecting shells, delighted when a pod
of dolphins breached and played across the broad
beachfront. If I could have any wish

it would be this: that this day and this night
would replay every day, every night.

M. Brooke Wiese's work has appeared most recently in *The Road Not Taken, Spoon River Poetry Review, The Orchards Poetry Journal, Sparks of Calliope, Poem*, and in *Poetry Porch*. Her chapbook, *At the Edge of The World*, was published by The Ledge Press in 1999, and her sonnets have been taught by poet Billy Collins to his college students, as well as anthologized and nominated for a Pushcart Prize. After a very long hiatus she has been writing furiously again. She writes in traditional forms on contemporary subjects in a modern voice. She lives with her wife and sons in New York City, has worked in education and nonprofit social services, and currently teaches English at a special education inclusive school in Manhattan, to high school students of all abilities.

www.ingramcontent.com/pod-product-compliance
Lightning Source LLC
Chambersburg PA
CBHW022043080426
42734CB00009B/1223